THE
COLLABORATIVE
Artist

Curiouser and Curiouser

by NANCY FABER

FLUTE

VIOLIN

PIANO

This work was originally commissioned by
Music Teachers National Association in celebration of its
Year of Collaborative Music — 2011

FABER
PIANO ADVENTURES®

ISBN 978-1-61677-703-6

"Curiouser and curiouser!"

~Alice, *Alice's Adventures in Wonderland,*
  by Lewis Carroll

Curiouser and Curiouser
for Flute, Violin, and Piano

Quick and curious (♩ = 120-132)

Nancy Faber
(b. 1955)

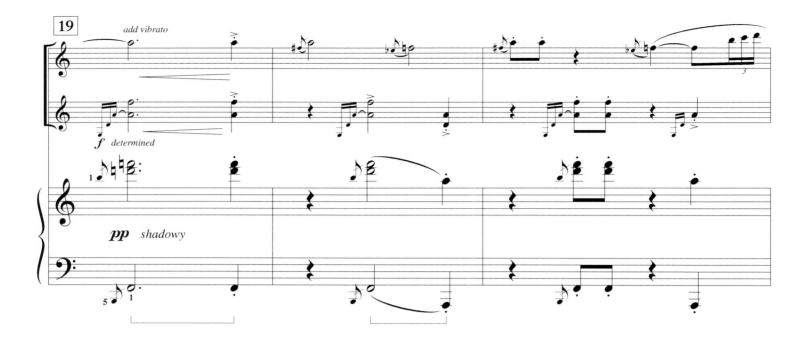

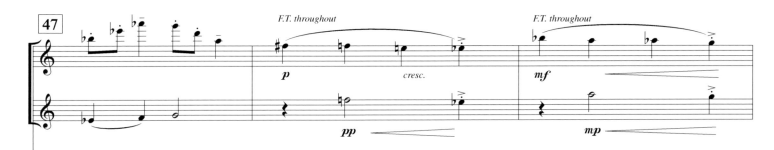

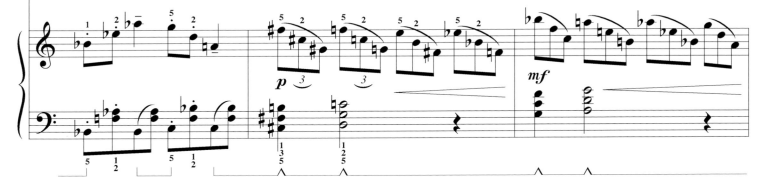

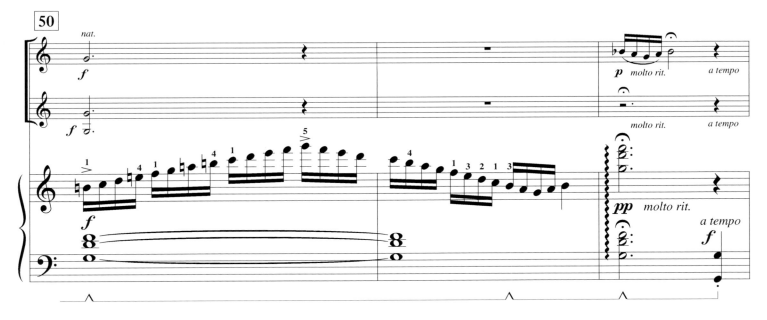

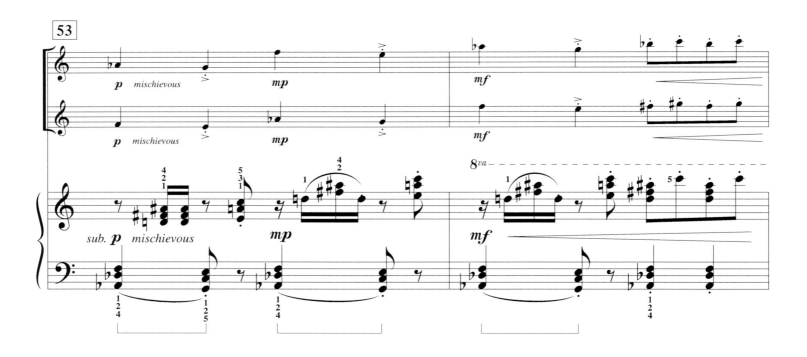

Flute

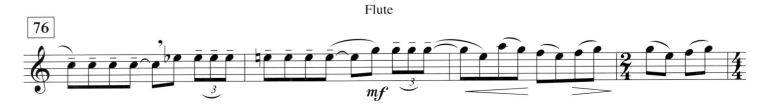

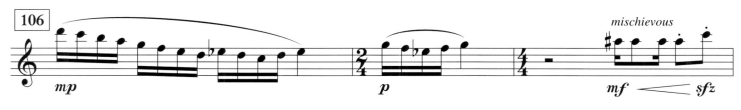

Flute

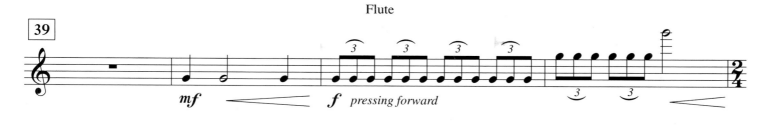

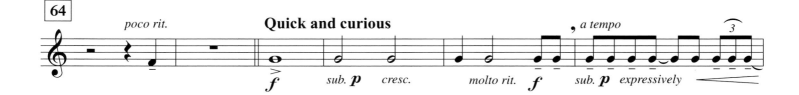

Curiouser and Curiouser
for Flute, Violin, and Piano

Nancy Faber
(b. 1955)

Flute

Quick and curious (♩ = 120-132)

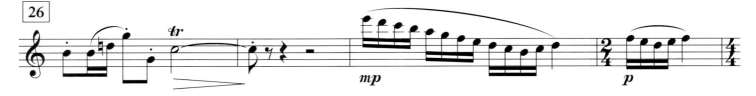

Violin

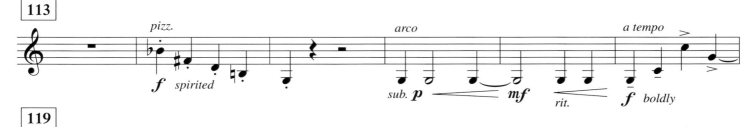

135 **Quick and curious**

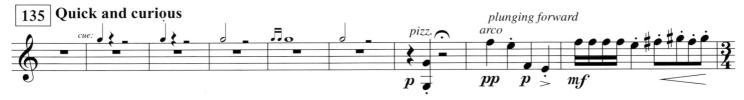

FF7003-Vln

66 **Quick and curious**

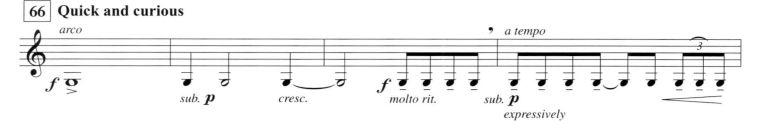

70

73

76

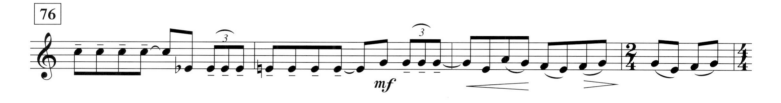

80

84

88

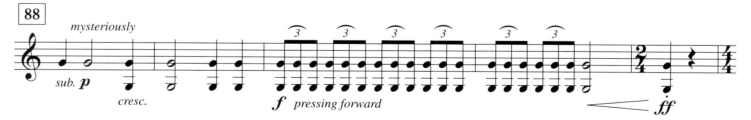

93

Violin

Curiouser and Curiouser
for Flute, Violin, and Piano

Violin

Nancy Faber
(b. 1955)

Quick and curious (♩ = 120-132)

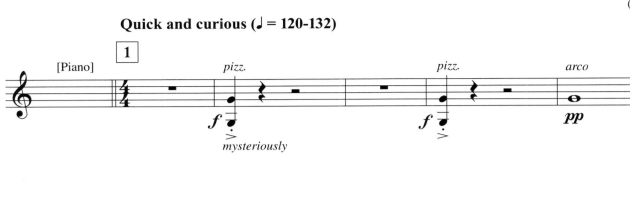

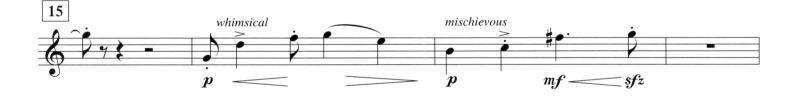

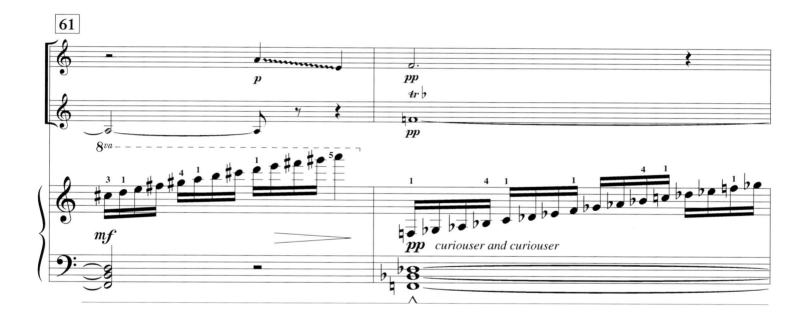

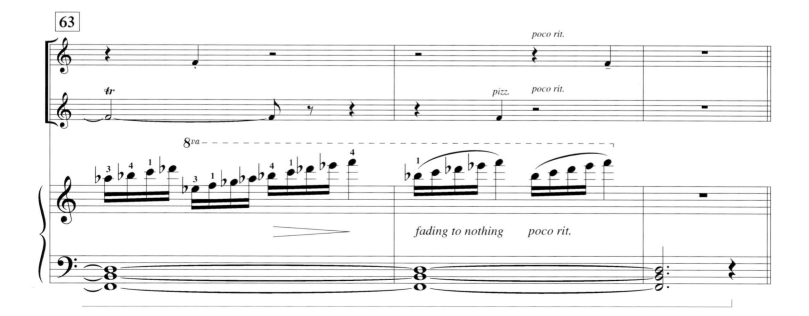

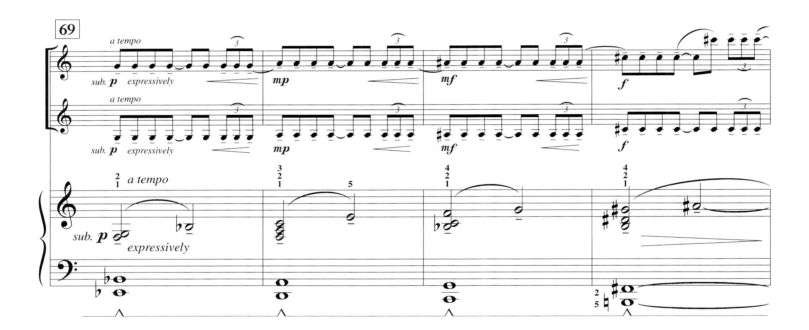

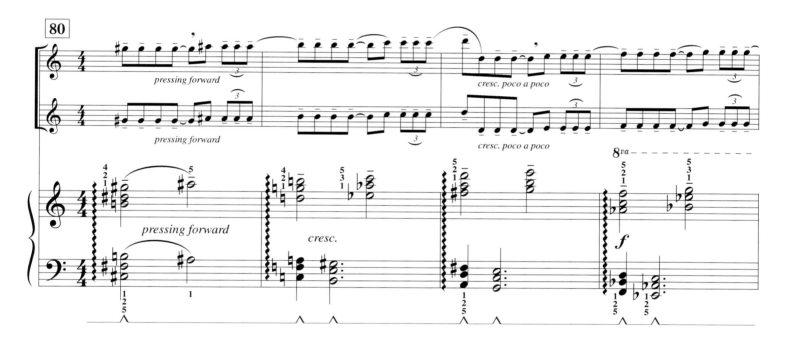

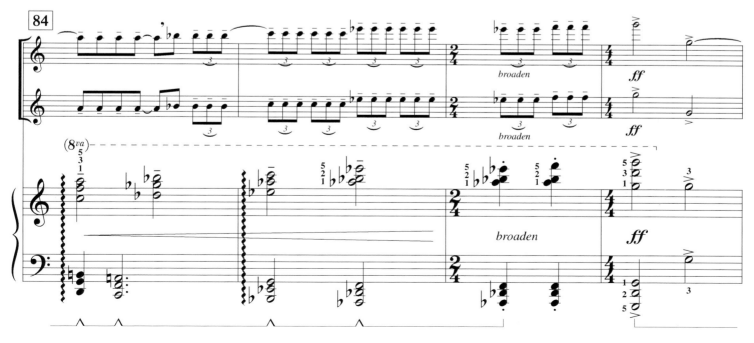

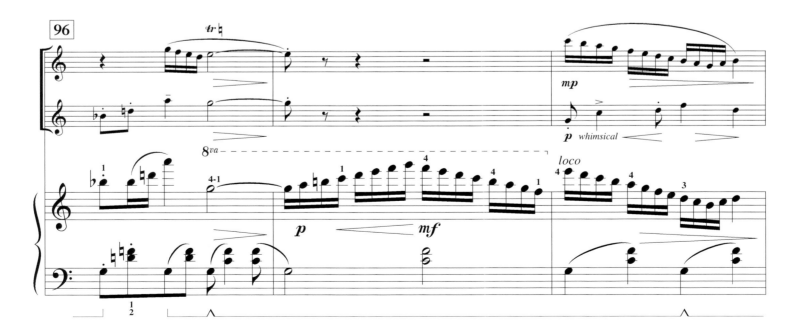

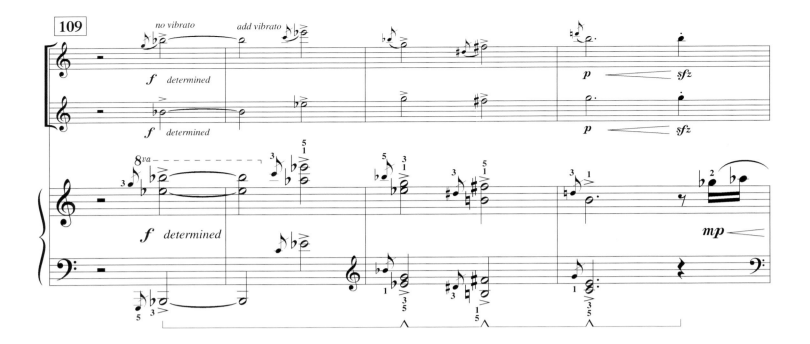

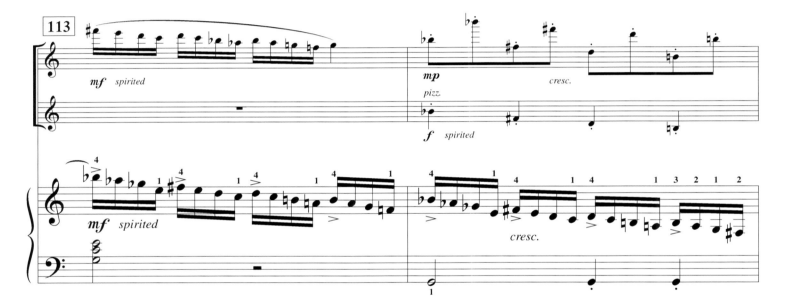

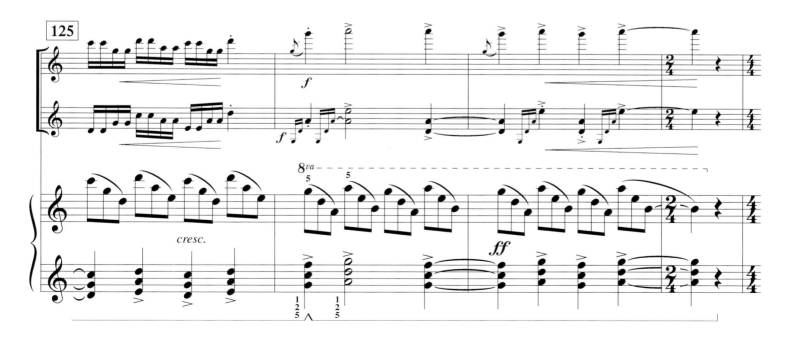

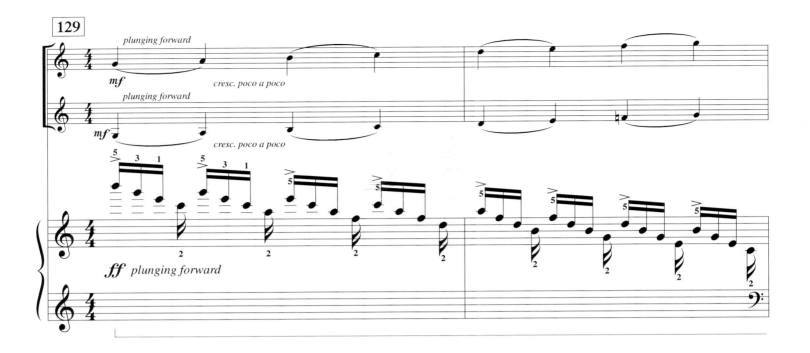